E.S.E.A. Chapter 2 1995
Clay Community Schools

15872

977
MOR   Morgan, Nina

                The Mississippi

DUE DATE	BRODART	01/95	22.80

RIVERS OF
THE WORLD

THE MISSISSIPPI

Nina Morgan

photographed by Laurence Fordyce

RSVP
RAINTREE
STECK-VAUGHN
PUBLISHERS
The Steck-Vaughn Company

Austin, Texas

Cover: A huge steel arch dominates the St. Louis skyline.

Series editor: Rosemary Ashley
Series designer: Derek Lee
Editorial and design: Paul Bennett
Cover design: Scott Melcer

Library of Congress Cataloging-in-Publishing Data

Morgan, Nina.
  The Mississippi / Nina Morgan : photographed by Laurence Fordyce.
     p.   cm. — (Rivers of the world)
  Includes bibliographical references (p.   ) and index.
  Summary: An overview of the Mississippi River, its physical features, plants, and wildlife, history, explorers, role as a transportation route, and future.
  ISBN 0-8114-3103-7
  1. Mississippi River—Juvenile literature.   2. Mississippi River Valley—Juvenile literature.   [1. Mississippi River. 2. Mississippi River Valley.]   I. Fordyce, Laurence, ill. II. Title.   III. Series: Rivers of the world (Austin, Tex.)
F351.M75   1994   92-39950
977—dc20   CIP
                                                    AC

Typeset by Multifacit Graphics, Keyport, NJ
Printed in Italy by G. Canale C.S.p.A.
Bound in the United States by Lake Book, Melrose Park, IL
1 2 3 4 5 6 7 8 9 0 LB 99 98 97 96 95 94

RIVERS OF THE WORLD

CONTENTS

1
The Crookedest River in the World

The Native Americans called it Misi-sipi, meaning "Big Water." The author Mark Twain dubbed it the "crookedest river in the world." The black slaves in the South called it Old Devil River, or old Al (short for alligator). To the people who live along its banks it is known as Old Muddy, Old Man River, or simply the Mighty Mississippi. But under any name, the river today provides an important transportation route for a wide variety of goods. It is now one of the busiest commercial waterways in the world, carrying more than 600 million tons of cargo each year.

The Mississippi is at the center of a vast water transportation network. The network allows many types of goods to be transported cheaply from the center of the United States to ports all over the world. Ships can travel for nearly 1,800 miles along the Mississippi, all the way from Minneapolis in the north to the Gulf of Mexico in the south.

In addition, the tributaries, or rivers that flow into the Mississippi, bring in goods from as far away as Pittsburgh in the east, Sioux City in the west, and Chicago in the north. From the Gulf of Mexico, ships can gain access to the busy ports of the Atlantic coast. Tugs push huge convoys of barges up and down the river.

The American writer and humorist Samuel Langhorne Clemens, better known as Mark Twain, made the river famous in his stories about the adventures of Tom Sawyer and Huckleberry Finn. The Mississippi has captured the imagination of, and provided inspiration for, many people. A raft trip down the Mississippi gave President Abraham Lincoln his first glimpse of the cruel realities of slavery and made him determined to free the slaves. For the millions of people who live near the Mississippi, it is a way of life, providing recreation, employment, and prosperity.

A huge convoy of barges is pushed by a tug past the town of Cairo, Illinois.

2
A River in Old Age

The Mississippi River began its life around 20 million years ago during the Pleistocene ice age, when glaciers covered much of North America. Its source is Lake Itasca, a small lake in northwestern Minnesota, one of the many lakes left behind when the glaciers retreated.

The entire Mississippi basin—the area of land with rivers draining into the Mississippi—was once part of the Gulf of Mexico. Sixty-five million years ago, the place where Cairo, Illinois, is now situated (nearly 500 miles inland), was on the edge of the sea. Gradually, the Mississippi basin was filled in by a fine deposit of mud or sand from the retreating glaciers and sediments carried by the river system itself. Over its long history, the river has deposited a 3-mile thick pile of sediments near the present-day coastline.

Above Lake Itasca, the source of the mighty Mississippi River.

A cross section along the length of the Mississippi. The river travels relatively slowly for most of its journey.

Mtrs	Feet	0	500	1,000	1,500	2,000	2,500	3,000	3,500	4,000 **km**
		0	310	620	930	1,240	1,550	1,860	2,170	2,480 **miles**

Cross section along the length of the Mississippi

Lake Itasca

Minneapolis & St Paul

St Anthony's Falls

450 | 1,475

St Louis

Cairo

Memphis

Baton Rouge

New Orleans

Gulf of Mexico

Mark Twain called the Mississippi "the crookedest river in the world." Here the river twists and turns as it flows past Cairo, Illinois.

Traveling sediments

Today, large amounts of sediments from the western part of the drainage basin are carried south by the Mississippi. Some of the sediments are deposited along the way to provide rich soil for farms in Mississippi, Tennessee, Missouri, and Louisiana. The rest of the sediments flow on to the Gulf of Mexico, where they are deposited on the Mississippi Delta.

The Mississippi ranks among the top ten rivers in the world in terms of the amount of water and sediment carried. More than 470 million cubic yards of sediments, along with more than 416,072 gallons of water flow into the Gulf of Mexico each year from the Mississippi.

7

Key

~ Mississippi River

᷊ᨓ᷊ Delta area

A map showing the vast area of the Mississippi drainage basin.

A classic case of "old age"

A river in the early stages of its journey produces steep-sided valleys as it cuts its way through the land. Farther along on its course, the valleys become wider as the river loops and curls, or meanders, to find the path along which it can flow most easily. Such a river is said to be in "old age." The Mississippi is a classic example of a river in old age.

Each new twist and turn of the river means that its length is constantly changing, so that no one can be sure exactly how long the Mississippi River is. Estimates of the mighty river's length range from between 2,348 miles and 2,553 miles.

The drainage basin

The drainage basin of the Mississippi is so large that all of France could be fitted into it six times over. It covers more than 40 percent of the land area of the United States, and includes parts of thirty-one states and two Canadian provinces.

Along its length, the Mississippi is joined by the Missouri River, which drains the prairies and drier regions to the west, and the Ohio River, which flows through the forests and rich fields of the Corn Belt, to the east. Other major rivers that flow into the Mississippi include the Illinois from the east, and the Arkansas and Ouachita rivers from the west.

Barges line the banks of the Mississippi River north of New Orleans. A bridge allows traffic to cross the river.

Mississippi Facts

Area of the drainage basin: approximately 1,243,306 square miles.
Length of the Mississippi: constantly changing, but estimated to be between 2,348 and 2,553 miles. It forms, with the Missouri River, the world's third longest river system
Maximum width: 4,500 feet near Cairo.
Minimum width: 10 feet near its source at Lake Itasca.
Maximum depth: 115 feet between Baton Rouge and New Orleans.
Minimum depth: 4 inches near its source at Lake Itasca.
Difference in height between the river's source and mouth: 1,475 feet.
Amount of flow: 453,500 million cubic yards per day into the Gulf of Mexico.
Amount of sediment carried: 470 million cubic yards per year into the Gulf.
Area of the Delta: roughly 9,225 square miles of land above sea level. The Delta is extending into the Gulf of Mexico at a rate of 315 feet per year but, at the same time, land is being lost from the Delta due to it sinking into the sea. The land area lost from the Delta is 35 square miles per year.

Left Large plantation houses, like this one near Vacherie, Louisiana, once lined the Lower Mississippi.

Below Cotton is a valuable crop grown along the banks of the Lower Mississippi. In the past, slaves used to pick the cotton. Today, modern machinery does the job.

From Minnesota to the Gulf

The character of the Mississippi reflects the differences in the landscape through which it flows and the amount and types of sediment that flow into it. Along its length the color of the water changes from green to a yellow-orange or reddish brown as it receives sediments carried in from different parts of the drainage basin. For example, the reddish brown color comes from red sandstone debris brought in from the mountains of Colorado by the Missouri River.

The course of the river can be divided into four main regions: the source area north of St. Paul, Minnesota; the Upper Mississippi, which flows north of the junction of the Missouri and the Ohio rivers; the Lower Mississippi, which extends as far south as Baton Rouge, Louisiana; and the Delta.

The Mississippi begins as a small, clear stream only 10 feet wide and 4 inches deep, fed by Lake Itasca. It travels northeastward at first, through a low countryside dotted with lakes and marshes before turning toward the south. Just north of St. Paul the elevation of the river drops by 72 feet as it passes through St. Anthony's Falls. Canals have been built to allow ships

and barges to travel past the Falls safely.

In the Upper Mississippi region, south of St. Paul, the river widens and flows between steep limestone cliffs. More than 500 tiny islands dot its sparkling surface. Here the river travels through a landscape of rolling hills, prairies, and marshlands. These fertile farmlands make up the Corn Belt, which includes the corn-growing region in Illinois, east of the river, and the vast wheat fields to the west.

The upper dam at St. Anthony's Falls in Minneapolis, Minnesota. Dams and canals have been built to allow ships to pass through the falls safely.

When "Big Muddy," the sediment-laden Missouri, joins the Mississippi from the west, north of St. Louis, Missouri, the Lower Mississippi begins. This is the Mississippi of Tom Sawyer and Huckleberry Finn, where graceful plantation houses can still be seen from the river. Here the Mississippi flows as a wide, brown flood, which can be more than 4,595 feet wide. Roughly 125 miles farther downstream, where the Ohio River joins the Mississippi from the east at Cairo, Illinois, the Mississippi swells to its fullest extent—more than 6,600 feet wide. This section of the river, with its shifting sandbanks, changing currents, and sudden mists, has wrecked many boats. The river here is so muddy that people often say it is "too thick to drink, but too thin to plow."

Mark Twain (1835–1910)

Mark Twain is one of America's most well-known and popular writers. His real name was Samuel Langhorne Clemens and he grew up in the small steamboat town of Hannibal, Missouri, beside the Mississippi. From childhood he loved the river, and his pen name comes from the riverboat worker's slang words for ''two fathoms deep.''

In his books *The Adventures of Tom Sawyer, Adventures of Huckleberry Finn,* and *Life on the Mississippi*, he presents a vivid picture of life along the river in the mid-nineteenth century. Here is a passage from *Life on the Mississippi:*

> ''The Mississippi is well worth reading about. It is not a commonplace river, but on the contrary is in all ways remarkable. . . . It seems safe to say that it is also the crookedest river in the world, since in one part of its journey it uses up one thousand three hundred miles to cover the same ground that the crow would fly over in six hundred and seventy-five.''

This is Huckleberry Finn describing a night journey along the river on a raft:

> ''This second night we run between seven and eight hours, with a current that was making over four mile an hour. We catched fish and talked, and we took a swim now and then to keep off sleepiness. It was kind of solemn, drifting down the big, still river, laying on our backs looking up at the stars, and we didn't ever feel like talking loud, and it warn't often that we laughed—only a little kind of a low chuckle. We had mighty good weather as a general thing, and nothing ever happened to us at all—that night, nor the next, nor the next.'' (From *Adventures of Huckleberry Finn.*)

The Corn Belt

A vast amount of corn is grown in this part of the country, particularly in Illinois near the Ohio River, where the rich, dark-gray soil and heavy rainfall suit the crop. Here, the fields stretch as far as the eye can see. The corn is not grown as food for people, but as food for pigs and other farm animals. During the harvest, it is not unusual to see up to a dozen harvesters spread across the open landscape.

The large volumes of water brought into the Mississippi from the Missouri and Ohio rivers make the Lower Mississippi very prone to flooding. The sediments carried by the floodwaters have, in the past, covered several cities, but they have also been spread over the land to provide rich soil for growing such crops as tobacco, cotton, rice, and peanuts.

The Delta begins at Baton Rouge, an industrial city nearly 155 miles north-west of the river mouth on the Gulf of Mexico. From here the river flows south among a tangle of canals, marshes, and complex branching streams, known as bayous. The river reaches its maximum depth of 115 feet over this part of the river, as it travels on its ever-changing course to the Gulf.

South of Baton Rouge, the river flows among a tangle of marshes, bayous, and islands.

3
Ecology and Wildlife

Because of the varied geography of the Mississippi there are many different types of habitats for water creatures and plants. It also attracts many land animals, who come to the river to drink or feed. Because the Mississippi has been around for a long time, a complex network of animal and plant communities has had time to develop. As a result, many unusual animals are found in this region of the country.

The Upper Mississippi

The clear waters of the Upper Mississippi travel through forests of hardwood trees, including basswood, hickory, maple, and oak. In this part of the country, fur trappers spent the winters trapping the many beavers that lived in and around the river, and hunted the deer, moose, and black bears that lived in the surrounding forests. Birds are also

White-tailed deer roam the forests near the Mississippi River at Bayou Black, Louisiana.

A salt marsh near Leville, Louisiana. Here the fresh water from the Mississippi mingles with salt water from the Gulf to provide a home for plants and animals that can adapt to the frequent changes of salinity in the water.

important inhabitants in and around the river. The loon, the "state bird" of Minnesota, is a common sight along the river's course.

The clear waters of the Upper Mississippi supports a large fish population. Fish such as bass, sunfish, and trout, which prefer sediment-free waters, thrive here. These fish are caught for both sport and food.

The Lower Mississippi

South of Cairo the nature of the forest changes. Here, trees such as bald cypress, southern oak, and tupelo, which prefer a warmer, wetter environment, are common. Fish that can tolerate silty waters thrive in this muddy part of the Mississippi. These include carp, catfish, and buffalo fish.

15

The Delta

The network of swamps and bayous in the Delta is home to many unusual plants and animals. In this watery environment, the dominant vegetation is a type of cypress specially adapted for life in the swamps. Other trees include white cedars, broad-leaved evergreens, and a type of rubber tree. Orchids—plants have flowers of unusual shapes and beautiful colors—grow freely here, and there are many giant and carnivorous types that consume insects.

In this freshwater swamp near Bayou Black, Louisiana, a type of cypress specially adapted to grow with its roots in the water is the dominant type of tree.

Left Although pretty to look at, the water hyacinth is a serious pest in the Delta region, as it forms a thick mat over the surface of the water.

The American alligator is a common sight in the Delta bayous.

The water hyacinth, a plant first introduced in the United States in 1884 as a gift from the Brazilian people, has adapted so well that it has become a serious pest. It forms a thick mat of flowers and leaves over the surface of the Delta waters, that threatens to choke the habitat of the creatures that live there. The problem is so serious that the government has set up a program to control its spread.

The waters of the Delta are home to many unusual forms of reptiles, amphibians, and fish. Alligators are common, and fish and amphibians can grow to an enormous size here—some frogs are as big as footballs.

Paddlefish can grow up to 6 feet in length, and some of the sturgeons in the Delta are 10 feet long. Many of the fish, including a species of dogfish, can be found only in this region.

In prehistoric times, animals similar to elephants, called mastodons, roamed the Delta marshes. Today, land animals include coypu, a type of large rodent that lives in the undergrowth, as well as raccoons, river otters, bobcats, and white-tailed deer.

The Delta is an important habitat in the life cycle of many birds. More than three hundred species, ranging from eagles to waterfowl and hummingbirds, visit the Delta each year.

The ''Mississippi flyway''

Backwaters, or isolated areas of water, up and down the Mississippi attract large numbers of water birds, that fly by the river with the changing seasons. They are drawn to these quiet areas because of the abundance of food plants, such as sedges, pondweeds, and millets.

The birds travel along the ''Mississippi flyway,'' an aerial migration route which extends from their winter homes in the Delta to the summer nesting grounds in northern Canada. Typical migrants include Canada and lesser snow geese, a wide variety of ducks, including mallards, teals, blacks, widgeons, pintails, ring necks, and coots. An estimated eight million geese, ducks, and swans travel to the southern part of the flyway to spend the winter. Even more travel along it on their way south to Latin America.

Problems with pollution and people

Pollution from farms and industry along the Mississippi poses a serious threat to the wildlife. Since 1970, laws have been introduced to try to clean up the river and prevent further damage.

In the Delta region, the digging of canals to provide routes through the dense swamplands is disrupting the delicate ecological balance of the region. Increasingly, garbage is being dumped in the swamps. People living near the Mississippi face some hard choices in their struggle to earn a living without damaging their fragile and unique environmental setting.

Huge flocks of Canada geese travel along the ''Mississippi flyway'' on their way to their summer nesting grounds in northern Canada.

18

4
The Early Explorers

Hernando de Soto, the first European to visit the Mississippi. De Soto was searching for gold, and reached the Mississippi River in 1541. He died in 1542, and was buried near the river.

From early times, the Native Americans traveled along the Mississippi River in their wooden canoes and fished from its waters. But European explorers did not discover the river until early in the sixteenth century.

Although a map of the New World made in 1507 by Christopher Columbus shows the mouth of the Mississippi, most people believe that the first European to visit the river was the Spanish explorer Hernando de Soto, who came to the New World in search of gold. In 1541, after a difficult journey west from Florida, he arrived at the Mississippi, a river so wide he could hardly see across it. De Soto named it the Rio Grande, or Big River. De Soto died during his quest for gold, and was buried near the river he discovered.

Europeans did not visit the Mississippi again until 1673, when two French explorers, Louis Jolliet and Jacques Marquette, set out from Quebec in Canada in search of a good east-west trade route. They explored the source of the Mississippi, and traveled downstream as far as the mouth of the St. Francis River in the present-day state of Arkansas. When they realized the river ran from north to south, they gave up.

However, another French explorer Sieur de La Salle, was quick to see the strategic importance of the Mississippi no matter which direction it flowed. After traveling from the Great Lakes to arrive at the Delta in 1682, he claimed the entire Mississippi basin for France. He named the territory Louisiana, after the French King Louis XIV.

Spanish explorers also claimed land around the Mississippi, but the largest settlements were established by the French. In 1718, Jean Baptiste Le Moyne founded New Orleans about 105 miles from the sea. Soon it was the largest city on the river. The Mississippi became a vital link between the French territories near the Delta and the settlements in Canada.

Meriwether Lewis and William Clark set out from St. Louis, Missouri, in 1804, to try to find a route to the Pacific Ocean. On their journey they had many encounters with Native Americans.

Right After Lewis and Clark returned with exciting tales of the land to the west, hundreds of people set off in wagon trains to travel there in search of a better life.

Left A huge steel arch on the banks of the Mississippi commemorates the role of St. Louis, Missouri, as the "Gateway to the West."

The "Gateway to the West"

In 1783, the Mississippi River was declared to be the western boundary of the newly formed Untied States. But the growing United States was not confined by the river for long. In 1803, President Thomas Jefferson purchased the Louisiana Territory from the French for fifteen million dollars.

In 1804, the American explorers Meriwether Lewis and William Clark set out from St. Louis to explore the new territory, and try to find a route to the Pacific Ocean. When they returned two years later full of exciting tales of the land to the west, hundreds of people flocked to St. Louis, hoping to join a wagon train to travel there in search of a better life. In spite of the many hazards of the journey, the land in the west was free to anyone who built a house and registered a claim for the land. St. Louis became the supply and setting-off point for the journey, but many settlers decided to stay. Today, a huge steel arch dominates the St. Louis skyline and commemorates the city's role as the "Gateway to the West."

With the arrival of steamboats on the Mississippi in 1811, it became possible to ship goods upriver, as well as downstream. Steamboat races became a popular entertainment.

The steamboat era

The Mississippi had long been a vital transportation route for people living along the river, but originally transportation was mainly downstream, with the flow of the river, from north to south. When the first steamboat, *The New Orleans,* appeared on the Mississippi in 1811, the river took on a new importance. Now goods could be easily shipped upstream as well as downstream.

The steamboat era led to great wealth wealth for the towns along the river that competed to service the steamboats. By 1840, New Orleans had become the fourth largest port in the world, and handled as many goods as New York.

The railroads made it possible for goods to be transported over land. As a result, the amount of cargo handled by the steamboats dropped dramatically.

The Civil War

At the time of the Civil War, fought between the North and South between 1861 and 1865 over the issue of slavery, commercial steamboat traffic on the river stopped. Instead, the river became a military objective. When the Northern army gained control of the Mississippi at Vicksburg, this marked the beginning of the end for the Southern troops. As a result of the Northern victory, slavery became illegal throughout the United States.

The coming of the railroad

After the end of the Civil War, there was a revival in river traffic. The Mississippi became an important commercial route once again.

The building of the Eads Bridge across the Mississippi at St. Louis in 1874 marked the beginning of the end for steamboat cargoes on the Mississippi. The railroad made it possible to ship goods overland to and from the East Coast. This meant that it was no longer necessary to ship these goods down the

Plantation Slaves

From the sixteenth century, thousands of people were forced from their homes in Africa to work as slaves on the sugar, tobacco, and cotton plantations in the South. Many of the slaves were treated like animals—they had no rights and the slave owners had the power of life and death over them. It was not until 1865, the end of the Civil War, that slavery became illegal throughout the United States.

A large oil tanker travels along the Mississippi near New Orleans. It is carrying oil from the refineries at Baton Rouge to the port of New Orleans for shipment around the world.

Mississippi and around the southern coast of the United States by sea.

The steamboat towns became quiet. By 1910, the amount of cargo handled by steamboats at St. Louis had dropped to just 10 percent of that handled only fifty years before.

During World War I (1914–1918), when other routes for moving materials for the war effort became crowded or difficult, the government supported the organization of new barge companies on the Mississippi, and operated dredges to keep shipping channels open. Once again the river flourished as a transportation route.

By 1931, the Mississippi carried twice as much traffic than it had ever carried in its history. World War II (1939–1945) provided an additional stimulus to river traffic as the Mississippi carried necessary military goods and materials. Today, traffic on the Mississippi continues to grow, and the river is one of the most active and important commercial waterways in the world.

5

Transportation Today

Barge convoys

The only steamboats seen on the river now operate for tourists. Today, huge convoys of barges linked together by steel clamps and pushed by powerful tugs are the main river traffic. Some of these convoys are up to one mile long, and are made up of barges arranged three or four together.

Many types of goods are carried along the Mississippi by the convoys. These include agricultural products, coal, iron, sand, oil, and industrial goods. Booster rockets for space research once traveled on barges down the Mississippi because they were too bulky to transport in any other way. Barge convoys are the cheapest way to transport vast amounts of cargo. It would take a 4-mile-long train to carry the weight of goods transported by one large barge convoy.

Most barges are built for specific types of cargoes. Barges for dry cargo are usually 190 feet long and 30 feet wide. Barges designed for carrying liquid cargoes are even larger: around 295 feet long and 50 feet wide. They require a water depth of more than 8 feet to travel safely.

Left and below Sturdy tugs, with specially designed flat bows, push huge convoys of barges up and down the Mississippi.

Intracoastal Waterway

The Mississippi transportation system is linked to the intracoastal waterway, which runs along the coast of the Gulf of Mexico. This series of dredged channels allows large ships year-round access to ports around the Gulf, both to bring in raw materials for industry and to carry away goods for shipment to ports around the world. As a result, industrial activity has become an important source of income for cities near the Gulf ports. Industries include oil refineries, chemical plants, and smelters for imported metal ores.

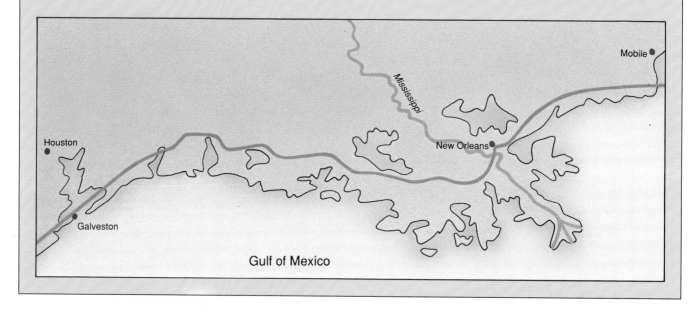

Cargo facilities

Cargo facilities on the riverbank have changed over the years. For example, where once New Orleans had ships docked several deep, waiting to unload their cargoes into warehouses, now huge cranes lift giant cargo containers off the convoys directly on to tractor trailers to continue the journey by land.

Navigating the river

From the early days of transportation on the Mississippi, navigation has been difficult. Hidden sandbanks can ground ships. The shape of the Mississippi is ever changing, and a channel that is deep enough to take big ships one day may be a sandbank the next.

In 1879 the government set up the Mississippi River Commission to try to control flooding and improve navigation on the river. Improvements are still being made to increase the value of the Mississippi as a transportation route. Today, a 40-foot-deep channel now runs from the mouth of the Delta as far as Baton Rouge. A 13-foot-deep channel continues as far north as Vicksburg. From the ocean traffic terminals at New Orleans and Baton Rouge, 9-foot-deep channels now extend up the river as far as Minneapolis and into the tributaries to form an extensive shipping network inside the United States.

In spite of the many improvements made to the shipping channels in the river, the strong currents and flooding that caused so many problems for the old steamboats continue to make travel difficult for the barge convoys today. Sometimes high waves on the river upset the cargoes on the barges, or push whole convoys off course with such strength that it takes the boat workers a great deal of skillful maneuvering for them to get back on course.

Because of these dangers, no shipper would allow a boat or convoy to leave a river port without a pilot on board to direct the navigation. The pilots are experts who know all the details of the river. With the aid of modern electronic devices, such as ship-to-shore radio, radar, and electronic depth finders, the pilots are able to safely guide the convoys to their destinations.

Right Bright orange markers are used to mark the channels where it is safe for ships to travel.

Below Barge convoys can be up to one mile long.

Terry and Deb Lownes

"We have been fishing the Mississippi all our lives. There are many different types of fish in the river—yesterday we caught a striped bass and some catfish. We have seen lots of changes. About thirty years ago, the government started building dams to control the river and, as a result, a series of lakes were formed. The lakes flooded many of the small islands and people who lived on them were forced to move. Our aim is to fish the whole of the Mississippi— from Lake Itasca all the way to the Gulf of Mexico."

The Mid River Service

The people who man the boats or convoys often travel with their cargoes for days and nights without stopping before they reach their port of destination. The Mid River Service, a fleet of small patrol boats, travels out to mid-channel to meet the tankers and deliver groceries and mail, and take orders for supplies.

The versatile river

The valley of the Mississippi is called the granary of the United States. The river provides water for crops, and much of the rich soil in the fertile farmland close to the Mississippi was deposited as the river flooded the land. The river also provides a cheap and convenient means of transporting the crops to market.

Dams, such as this one near Clarksville, Missouri, help to control the water level on the Mississippi.

Large tanks, known as elevators, are used to store grain carried south from the grain and corn growing regions along the Upper Mississippi River at the Port of Rosedale, Mississippi.

Since the first mills were established near Minneapolis, in the middle of the nineteenth century, to take advantage of the water power generated by St. Anthony's Falls, the Mississippi has been used to fuel industry. Water from the river can provide a useful source of power. Also, water is an essential ingredient for industrial processes such as oil refining. It takes roughly 1,930 gallons of water to refine one barrel of crude oil. The easy access to water from the river has helped Baton Rouge to become a major oil terminal.

Chuck Miller

"I am a personnel manager for a shipping line here at Vacheree in Louisiana. To the men who work on the barges, I am known as the Port Captain, and I am responsible for working out the wages, supplying groceries and other items that the deckhands need on a long trip, interviewing applicants for jobs, and so on. I manage forty people, who transport coal on barges to ports up and down the Mississippi. The barges are lashed together individually, using steel cables 35 feet long. That way a single barge can be released from the convoy without too much trouble at any port on the river."

6

Mississippi Ports

Many cities along the banks of the Mississippi became regional trading centers, and grew wealthy by serving as ports for the boats that transported goods along the river.

Minneapolis and St. Paul

The most northerly of the important port cities are the twin cities of Minneapolis and St. Paul, which are located near St. Anthony's Falls. Until the early 1900s, when the U.S. Army Corps of Engineers built a system of locks to allow boats to travel through the Falls, these cities were the end of the line for river traffic heading north.

Minneapolis, located on the west bank of the river, is a major railroad center for the northwest, and is an important center for the buying and selling of grain. Its port handles more than 2.5 million tons of goods, including large cargoes of logs, which are floated down the river from the north. Another 11 million tons of goods pass through the port facilities of St. Paul on the east bank.

St. Louis

The city of St. Louis began in 1764 as a small French settlement on the west bank of the Mississippi. Originally, it served as a trading post for furs, which were shipped down the Mississippi to New Orleans. With the coming of the steamboats around 1817, the city grew quickly. The steamboats moored three and four deep along the riverbank, and St. Louis became a center for the transportation of goods and passengers. The steamboats are now a tourist attraction and are used as restaurants.

More than 29 million tons of goods are handled at St. Louis each year; most are destined for other domestic ports.

The twin cities of Minneapolis and St. Paul are centers for shipping and commerce.

St. Louis is an important Mississippi port, and supports a strong communications industry.

Baton Rouge is an important center for oil refineries, and is the fourth most active port in the United States.

Memphis

Memphis is the first big commercial port on the route down the Mississippi. The city of Memphis, Tennessee, was established in 1819. With the hard work of slaves, who drained swamps and cleared land in the nineteenth century, it became the center of the cotton industry, a position it still holds today. More than 12 million tons of goods are handled at Memphis every year.

Baton Rouge

Baton Rouge, the capital of Louisiana, is surrounded by the highly productive oil fields of the Delta region. This has helped to make it a major industrial center and home to one of the largest oil processing complexes in the world. Barges load up the refined oil tanks, which line the riverbank, and carry petroleum products downstream to New Orleans.

Baton Rouge is the fourth busiest port in the United States, and is the farthest inland of all the deep-water ports serving the Gulf of Mexico. Baton Rouge is an international port—of the 79 million tons of goods that pass through it each year, 28 million tons are destined for foreign ports.

New Orleans

Although New Orleans is located 100 miles inland from the Gulf of Mexico, because of a series of canals and inland waterways it serves as the port of entry to the entire interior of the United States. In the past, the port of New Orleans received goods such as cotton, grain, and livestock, which were exported to many parts of the world. Today, trade is dominated by products made from oil.

New Orleans is an international port, second only to New York in terms of the total amount of shipping in numbers of tons and value of exports. More than 175 million tons of goods pass through New Orleans each year and, of these, 66 million tons are imports and exports. Increased trade between the United States and countries in Latin America means that the port of New Orleans is continuing to grow. In addition to its importance as a port, New Orleans has a rapidly-growing region of industry developing around it.

A new port facility, Centroport USA, is being developed in New Orleans, to move some of the port's activities away from the Mississippi to wharves and industrial complexes along the Gulf Coast.

Opposite New Orleans is the second largest port in the United States. It serves as the main port of entry for goods destined for the interior of the country.

New Orleans, the Birthplace of Jazz

The old part of the city of New Orleans, the French Quarter, is a popular place to visit. This is where jazz was born, and famous musicians, such as Louis Armstrong, rose to fame.

Mardi Gras, or "fat Tuesday," in New Orleans, is one of the most famous celebrations in the United States. This takes place just before the Christian fasting period of Lent starts on Ash Wednesday, and people come from all over the world to see the colorful and noisy street parades, dancing, and masquerade parties.

Even when Mardi Gras has ended, the city is full of music, which can be heard drifting out of the bars and cafés.

7
Conquering the Mississippi

The most outstanding characteristic of the Mississippi is its unpredictability. The river level can change suddenly, and flooding occurs regularly. And the changing course of the river means that a channel may be deep enough for shipping one day, but a hazardous sandbank the next.

The Mississippi River Commission

As early as 1717, settlers were building embankments or levees to try to protect their riverside farms from flooding. In the nineteenth century, Mark Twain described how the steamboat captains would band together to exchange infor-

In spite of the great amount of engineering work carried out to prevent flooding, floods are still a fact of life for many people living near the Mississippi.

mation about the changing conditions along the channel. Since 1879, flood protection and the provision of navigational information have been the job of the Mississippi River Commission.

To help in its work, the Commission has constructed a working scale model of the river over a several acre site in Vicksburg. Engineers working to control floods on the Mississippi use this model to test their ideas before putting them into practice. To help them they use photographs taken by aircraft and satellites, and information about sediments laid down by the river, which they gather from drilling holes. By creating artificial floods in the model, the scientists aim to avoid disastrous floods like the one in 1973, that left almost 70 million acres of land along the Mississippi and its tributaries under water, and millions of dollars worth of damage.

Controlling the floods

The water level in the Mississippi varies widely. Variations in the river's flow are linked with rainfall in the Mississippi basin and the variable amounts of water that are carried into the Mississippi by the rivers that drain into it, such as the Missouri and the Tennessee.

Rainfall is heaviest in the Mississippi basin in the late spring and early summer. At this time, the water level rises dramatically, and its rate of discharge into the Gulf can more than double. The Ohio is chiefly responsible for the flooding which occurs in the Lower Mississippi. Flooding occurs especially when there are early rains in the Great Plains, a sudden hot spell which melts the snow in the north, heavy rains in the lower valley, and the Ohio is at maximum flow.

To help in their work of controlling flooding and keeping shipping routes open, the Mississippi River Commission has constructed several scale models of the river.

Preventive and defensive measures

To control the flooding and prevent damage, the U.S. Army Corps of Engineers uses both defensive and preventive measures. To prevent flooding in the first place, it aims to control the way rainfall runs off the land and into the Mississippi and its tributaries. One way of doing this is to establish a thicker cover of plants and trees, which would encourage the rainfall to soak into the ground, rather than quickly draining into the rivers. When the early settlers cleared the forests and land for farming, they created a situation where erosion and, therefore flooding was more likely to happen.

Defensive measures include building high banks and levees along the river to confine it to its channel. These can take the form of massive walls of reinforced concrete rising 3 to 10 feet above the river. From just north of Cairo, a 942-mile stretch of the Lower Mississippi is lined by tremendous levees, walls more than 1,985 miles long. In its entirety, 1,085 miles of the river now runs in artificial channels.

In towns such as Cairo, the levees rise high above the streets. When the river rises to a dangerous level the openings in the levees are closed using heavy steel gates to prevent flooding.

If the main levees are threatened, the excess flood water is drained away down spillways. For example, north of New Orleans, the spillways divert flood water past the city directly into the Gulf of Mexico. The engineers have also designed especially weakened sections of the levees, known as "fuse plugs." These burst under excess pressure and allow the water to flow harmlessly into floodways or reservoirs. A fuse-plug system has been built at New Madrid, Missouri, which is located on the Mississippi, in the area just south of the junction with the Ohio River.

In other parts of the Mississippi, the banks have been protected against erosion and channels have been stabilized, using concrete blocks held together with massive cables. In addition, dikes have been built underwater to control the flow of the current, and channels are continuously dredged to keep them open to shipping and to maintain the free flow of water.

A high-water gauge near Cairo, Illinois.

Levees

Natural levees, or low embankments, build up along the banks of the Mississippi every time it floods. When the river overflows its banks, sediment is deposited at the edge of the channel and gradually builds up to form a low wall. Beyond the levees, the ground slopes downward, and tends to be marshy.

Although natural levees help to prevent flooding along the river, artificial levees are also needed. However, sometimes trying to prevent the flooding only leads to more trouble. When the river is confined by walls it sometimes begins to silt up. This causes the level of the riverbed to rise, and the danger of flooding becomes greater than before the levees were built.

Over the years, stronger and higher levees, up to 20 to 30 feet high, have been built to try to prevent flooding on the Mississippi. But the Mississippi will not be tamed, and flooding is still a danger.

Levees are built in some places to try to control flooding. In cities such as Cairo, Illinois, the levees rise high above the streets.

U.S. Army Corps of Engineers

The defenses against floods along the Mississippi are carefully planned and coordinated by the U.S. Army Corps of Engineers. Using the Vicksburg scale model, they aim to predict the extent of the largest flood possible along the valley of the Mississippi, and devise ways of preventing the spread of water, as well as protecting people and property.

In spite of all this effort, the river is still in control, and a delicate balance exists between safety and flooding. When one part of the Mississippi's course is altered or where levees are built to control flooding, the engineers must consider the effect this will have on other parts of the river.

Today, the risk of serious flooding on the Mississippi is not great. However, the U.S. Army Corps of Engineers maintains a constant watch on the river's progress.

Below Flooding along the Mississippi can be severe after storms. Here a helicopter helps in the rescue operation along the Mississippi after Hurricane Betsy struck in 1965.

Opposite In the Delta region of Louisiana, houses are built on stilts to keep them above the floodwaters.

8
The Delta

Delta geology

Deltas are flat areas of sediment. They occur at the mouths of rivers where the main stream of water slows down and divides up as it flows into the sea.

The Mississippi Delta we see today is only about 600 years old. It is the latest in a series of at least six deltas built up by the Mississippi since the last ice age, which ended around 10,000 years ago. The present-day Delta in Louisiana has a classic "bird's foot" shape. It is a good example of a river-dominated delta—one where the river has deposited more sediment than the tides and currents in the Gulf can carry away.

The shrinking Delta

When the sediment flow on a delta is reduced, the land area stops growing, and the delta tends to sink below the level of the sea under its own weight. This appears to be happening on the Mississippi Delta today.

Human interference to support commerce on the river is playing an important part in reducing the amount of sediment which reaches the Delta. Jetties at the mouth of the Mississippi route the sediment carried by the river directly out to deep water to prevent it from blocking shipping lanes. Because of this, the Delta is extending a further 315 feet into the Gulf of Mexico each year. In addition, soil conservation measures taken upstream are reducing the amount of sediment that flows on to the Delta. As a result, roughly 35 square miles of Delta land is being lost each year.

The Delta region is a complicated network of channels, streams, and islands.

The Delta wetlands

The Mississippi Delta is said to begin at Baton Rouge, but the wetlands, the region most characteristic of the Delta, extend only as far north as the region south of New Orleans. They cover an area of roughly 10,808 square miles in Louisiana, and support many unusual animal and plant communities. Relatively few people live in the wetlands, but those who do have a very unusual lifestyle.

Right For people in the Delta wetlands, fishing is a favorite sport, as well as an important way of earning a living.

Below The Isle St. Jean Charles in the Mississippi Delta region of Louisiana.

Delta people

These days, many of the Delta people live "up front" on strips of dry land that are protected from the Mississippi on one side, and the marshland on the other, by levees. Some of the residents also have houses in the marshlands, which they can reach only by boat.

41

Commercial fishers use nets to catch fish in the Delta.

There are still a few villages along the bayous where people live permanently. There, houses can only be reached by water, and a school boat collects children to take them to classes.

Delta communities can be very isolated and are often very closely knit. One resident described his hometown as: "Twenty-seven houses and one big happy family." Some Delta folk have never traveled farther away from home than the next village.

The people living in the wetlands come from many different backgrounds. The first Europeans to settle in the area were the Acadians, French-Catholics driven out of Nova Scotia, Canada, by the British in the late 1700s.

Allen Gillard

"I work at the coast guard station at Grand Island, which is very near to the Delta in the Gulf of Mexico. From here we operate the largest search and rescue area on the Gulf Coast, and last year we were called out 370 times. We are also responsible for investigating boats that may be carrying drugs into the country and for catching people who who are breaking the fishing laws. There are no emergency services on the island, and so we are often called out to fly sick or injured people to a mainland hospital by helicopter."

Large amounts of oil are present below the surface of the Delta. A tall derrick marks the site of a well which is being drilled to look for oil near Bayouneuf, Louisiana.

They were soon joined by other immigrants. The culture that developed in the bayou country is known as Cajun, a version of the name Acadian.

English is not the only language in use in the Delta region. The first settlers were French speaking, and a form of French known as Cajun-French is still spoken today. There are some Cajun-language radio stations broadcasting in this part of Louisiana. In addition, forms of Spanish, Croatian, and even Vietnamese can be heard here, reflecting the different cultural backgrounds of the people who now live on the Delta.

Delta industry

Fishing, particularly for shrimp, and farming crops, such as rice, which grows with its roots in the water, are traditional industries on the Delta. The abundance of good fresh seafood led to the development of a style of hot and spicy cooking known as Cajun, now popular throughout the world.

In recent years, many people on the Delta have found jobs working in the oil industry. Oil is abundant below the Delta's surface, and more than 22,000 oil wells have been drilled to recover it.

Canals

For many years, people have dug canals to allow them to travel through the dense marshes and swamps of the Delta. Now the oil industry wants to dig more canals to make transport and oil exploration easier. But there are some disadvantages to this proposal.

The canals provide an easy route for salt water from the Gulf of Mexico to penetrate the freshwater and brackish swamps and marshes. The plant and animal life of the Delta is already being affected by the inflow of salt water.

The measures taken to control the Mississippi are increasing the economic prospects for people who live in the region, but they are upsetting the natural geological and ecological balance of the Delta. The people of the Delta region face a difficult choice in trying to balance their commercial needs with those of the environment.

Left Products from this sugar refinery in Louisiana are shipped from nearby Mississippi ports.

Below This aerial photograph shows the shipping canals that have been cut straight through the marsh lands of the Delta.

Many Delta residents make their living by fishing. The unpredictable nature of the Mississippi and the digging of canals threatens this way of life.

The Mississippi has undergone many changes throughout its long history. Since its beginnings 20,000 years ago, as the glaciers that covered North America began to melt, the Mississippi has continuously changed its course. Today, the river is still altering its course—30 percent of its flow has now moved to the Atchafalaya River to the west.

In the last 150 years, people have begun to play an increasing role in the development of the river. But in spite of the best efforts of the Mississippi River Commission to control the river, flooding remains a constant danger, and it has proved to be a full-time job keeping shipping lanes open.

It is impossible for anyone to predict the course and nature of the river over the next thousand years. The Native Americans accepted the natural changes in the river. For the last 200 years, people have worked to control the Mississippi River. Now some people are beginning to wonder whether this is such a good idea.

Glossary

Amphibians Coldblooded animals that live on land and in water.

Backwaters Isolated areas of water connected to a river.

Basin The land drained by a river and its tributaries.

Brackish Slightly briny or salty water.

Cajun The name used to describe both the culture and people of the Delta region.

Carnivorous Certain plants that are able to trap and digest insects.

Communities Associations of plants and animals.

Containers Large, cargo-carrying, standard-sized containers that can be loaded from one mode of transportation to another.

Convoys Groups of barges or boats traveling together.

Delta The triangular stretch of land at the mouth of a river that reaches the sea in two or more branches.

Dikes Walls that prevent or control flooding.

Dredge To dig out or widen the course of a river.

Ecology The relationships between plants and animals and their natural surroundings.

Elevation Height above sea level.

Erosion The wearing or carrying away of sediments or rocks by the action of wind, water, or ice.

Evergreen A type of tree or shrub that bears leaves throughout the year.

Glaciers Slow-moving rivers of ice.

Habitats The natural homes of animals or plants.

Ice Age One of the several periods in the Earth's history when glaciers covered large areas of the land.

Limestone A type of rock formed from the material deposited by water, ice, or the wind.

Lock A part of a canal or waterway for raising or lowering boats.

Marshes Low-lying, wet ground.

Migration route The route used by animals and birds to journey between different habitats at certain times of the year.

Military objective A place or object that an army is trying to capture.

Navigational information Information about weather conditions, currents, and the position of sandbanks and other obstacles needed by ship's captains in order to make safe voyages.

Pleistocene An era in the geological timescale that ended around 10,000 years ago, and lasted for around 1.8 million years.

Prairies Stretches of level land, without trees and covered with grass.

Reptiles A group of coldblooded animals that include snakes, lizards, crocodiles, and tortoises.

Salinity The amount of salt in water.

Silt A fine deposit of, for example, sand or mud, in a river or lake.

Stategic To be in a well-placed situation.

Swamps Tree-covered areas where the ground is soft and saturated with water.

Terminals Sites where raw materials or goods are loaded or unloaded from ships.

Wetlands The unique freshwater swamp habitat in the Delta region.

BOOKS TO READ AND USEFUL ADDRESSES

Books to Read

Black, Patti, and Morrison, Ann, eds. *Walter Anderson for Children: An Activity Book from the Mississippi State Historical Museum.* Mississippi Archives

Crisman, Ruth. *The Mississippi* (First Book). Franklin Watts, 1984

Darell-Brown, Susan. *The Mississippi* (Rivers of the World). Silver Burdett, 1978

Hartford, John. *Steamboat in the Cornfield.* Crown, 1986

Lye, Keith. *Passport to the United States.* Franklin Watts, 1990

McCall, Edith. *Mississippi Steamboatman: The Story of Henry Miller Shreve.* Walker & Co., 1985

Rowland-Entwhistle, Theodore. *Rivers & Lakes* (Our World). Silver Burdett, 1987

Scarry, Huck. *Life on a Barge.* Prentice Hall, 1985

Twain, Mark. *Adventures of Huckleberry Finn.* Penguin Classics, 1985

Twain, Mark. *The Adventures of Tom Sawyer.* Penguin Classics, 1985

No Author. *Steamboats of the West (Frontiers of America).* Children's Press, 1980

For older readers

Keating, Bern. *The Mighty Mississippi.* National Geographic, 1979

O'Neil, Paul. *The Riverman.* Time-Life, 1975

Useful Addresses

For information about the Mississippi River write to:

The Mississippi River Commission
Lower Mississippi Valley Division
U.S. Army Corps of Engineers
P.O. Box 80
Vicksburg, MS 39181-80

Picture acknowledgments

All photographs including the cover by L. Fordyce/Eye Ubiquitous except the following: J. Allen Cash 24; Bruce Coleman Ltd. 33 (bottom)/Melinda Berge; Mary Evans Picture Library 12 (left); Geoscience Features 33; Peter Newark's Western Americana 12 (right), 19, 20, 21 (top), 22, 23 (both), 38. The map on page 5 is by Peter Bull Design. Artwork on pages 6, 8, and 31 is by John Yates.

INDEX

Numbers in **bold** refer to illustrations